DATE DUE

ENERGY FOREVER?

WATER POWER

IAN GRAHAM

RSVP

RAINTREE
STECK-VAUGHN
PUBLISHERS
A Steck-Vaughn Company

Austin, Texas

ENERGY FOREVER?

Water Power

OTHER TITLES IN THE SERIES

Solar Power · Wind Power · Fossil Fuels
Nuclear Power · Geothermal and Bio-Energy

Published by Raintree Steck-Vaughn Publishers,
an imprint of Steck-Vaughn Company

Library of Congress Cataloging-in-Publication Data
Graham, Ian.
Water power / Ian Graham.
    p.   cm.—(Energy Forever?)
Includes bibliographical references and index.
Summary: Examines historical uses of water as a source
of energy, the advantages and disadvantages, and new
advances in harnessing water power.
ISBN 0-8172-5363-7
1. Water power—Juvenile literature.
[1. Water power.]
I. Title. II. Series.
TC147.G67   1999
620.1'06—dc21   98-13438

Printed in Italy. Bound in the United States.
1 2 3 4 5 6 7 8 9 0 03 02 01 00 99

Picture Acknowledgments
Cover: Tony Stone/Getty Images/Tom Bean. Stockmarket: title page, 9,
20–21 (Ballantyne), 25 (Rose). U.S. Department of Energy: pages 4–5. Ole
Steen Hansen, Denmark: 5. Lionheart Books: 6–7. Eye Ubiquitous: 7
(NASA), title page, 16–17 (Brian Pickering), 41 (Steve Lindridge), 43
(Davy Bold). Ecoscene: 8–9 (Andrew Brown), 10 (Chris Knapton), 12–13
(Erik Shaffer), 13 (Andrew Brown), 14–15 (Richard Glover), 26 (Joan
Creed), 32 (Rob Nichol), 36 (Nick Hawkes), 40 (M. Jones). Mary Evans
Picture Library: 17, 19 (both), 20. AEA Technology: 22, 30, 30–31, 31,
34, 38–39. Samfoto: 28–29 (Jon Arne Sieter), 29 (Morten Loberg).
Kvaernar Brug, Norway: 32 (both). Canada House: 34–35. Frank Lane
Picture Agency/McCutcheon, Alaska, U.S.: 42–43. Illustrated by Rudi Vizi

CONTENTS

WHAT IS WATER POWER?

Introduction

Water power is the use of water to do work, such as producing electricity or driving mills. Water power is kinder to the environment than the burning of fossil fuels, in particular coal, oil, and gas, because it produces no air pollution or poisonous waste. Water is also a renewable resource—it can be used again and again.

A view of water gushing through the John Day Dam on the Washington-Oregon state line. It is one of several dams on the Columbia River that together provide more than 22,000 megawatts of electrical power to the Pacific northwest region of the United States.

Water-powered machines have been used for thousands of years, but the use of water power declined when cheap fossil fuels became more popular during the first half of the twentieth century. Steep increases in oil prices in the 1970s and greater concern about pollution have made water power more attractive once again.

Energy from running water is free. And it can be turned into useful work quite easily. While many water power projects use expensive new technology to make them as big and efficient as possible, simple handmade wooden machines can make use of water power, too. This book explores the history, the technology, the environmental impact, and the future of water power.

Above: Water cascades over the waterwheels at this Danish water mill. The mill is used to grind grain to make flour. Few water mills survive today, but once thousands of them lined the banks of rivers across Europe.

FACTFILE

About 6 percent of all the energy used by people comes from water-powered generators. Almost all of it is generated by hydroelectric power plants. The first water-powered machine that we know about is the water wheel. It was invented about 4,000 years ago in the Middle East, in the area we now call Turkey and Greece.

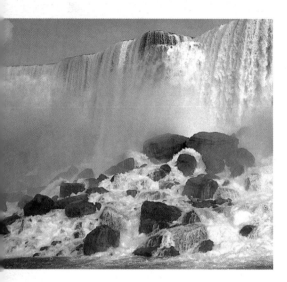

Above: The vast power potential of Niagara Falls on the U.S.-Canadian border was first tapped in 1757. Hydroelectric power plants at the falls now produce a flow of more than 4,000 megawatts of electricity—enough to supply the needs of a large city.

Where does water come from?

Water covers nearly three fourths of the earth's surface, but it was not always like this. When our planet was forming 4.6 billion years ago, water did not exist because it was so hot. As the earth cooled, atoms of hydrogen and oxygen gases linked to form water molecules. Vast clouds of water vapor swirled around the planet.

Scientists believe that when the earth cooled enough for the vapor to condense into water droplets, it may have rained all over the earth for hundreds of years! So much rain fell that the lowest parts of the planet filled with water to form the oceans. But the water did not stay there. Ever since those distant prehistoric times water has constantly moved around the earth in the clouds, rain, rivers, and oceans.

Water heated by the sun evaporates and rises into the atmosphere. Winds carry it to regions of cooler air where it condenses into water droplets, which fall as rain. The water flows down to rivers, lakes, and the sea, and the cycle begins again.

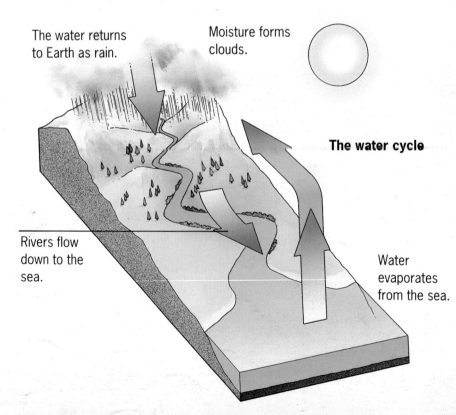

The water returns to Earth as rain.

Moisture forms clouds.

The water cycle

Rivers flow down to the sea.

Water evaporates from the sea.

Plants move vast quantities of water from the ground to the atmosphere. Water is drawn up into a plant through its roots. The water leaves the plant again by evaporating from microscopic holes in its leaves. A single oak tree can move 100 gal. (379 l) of water from the ground to the atmosphere in a day.

The earth is unique among the nine planets of the solar system. It is the only planet where water exists in its liquid form, with deep oceans as well as an oxygen-rich atmosphere with water vapor clouds.

Why is water so important?

Water is essential for life. The driest places on Earth are the places where there is the least life—the fewest plants and animals. The first forms of life on Earth developed in the sea. When plants and animals spread from the sea onto land, they continued to need water to survive. Green plants combine water and simple chemicals from the soil with carbon dioxide from the atmosphere to make food. Green plants are important because almost every other creature eats either plants or other creatures that themselves eat plants.

Plants grow only where they find water. In Israel's Negev Desert, plants grow along the edge of a seasonal stream. In places where underground water comes to the surface, green oases are formed.

More than half of the weight of a human being is water. We lose this water as perspiration, moisture in our breath, and when we go to the toilet. So we each have to replace more than half a gallon (2 l) of water every day. We drink about a quart (1 l) and the rest comes from our food. We can do without food for several weeks, but we can survive for only a few days without fresh water.

Water is also needed for industry, for washing, and for watering plants. Only 1 percent of all our water is freely available fresh water; 97 percent is salty water in the sea and the remaining 2 percent is fresh water locked underground and in glaciers and polar ice caps.

In nature, water always flows downhill under the force of gravity. If it is to be sent uphill or sprayed out of a hose, then it has to be pumped under pressure.

9

What causes the tides?

The sea level rises and falls about once every 12 hours. These daily changes in depth are known as the tides. The tides, which range from high to low sea levels and back again, are caused mainly by our closest neighbor in space, the moon. The moon is so close to us—only 248,555 mi. (400,000 km) away—that its gravity pulls strongly on the earth. It pulls water toward the side of the earth that is closest to it, causing high tides there.

Each day the tides are later than on the day before because the moon rises later each day. As it circles the spinning earth, the moon climbs above the horizon (the imaginary horizontal line between the sea and sky) about 50 minutes later every day, and the tides follow it. The sun affects the tides, too. The height of the tides depends on the positions of the sun, moon, and earth. The highest tides, called spring tides, occur at the full moon and new moon when the earth, moon, and sun all line up together.

F A C T F I L E

The tides—huge quantities of water moved around the earth by the moon's gravitation—have an important affect on world shipping. The captains of ships have to be sure when sea levels are deep enough for them to sail into ports or to follow certain sea routes. In some places, high tide can be 16 ft. (5 m) above low tide.

Here, as the sun sets, the moon rises over the Mediterranean island of Corsica. The changing positions of the earth and these two heavenly bodies are responsible for the daily rise and fall of tides around our coasts.

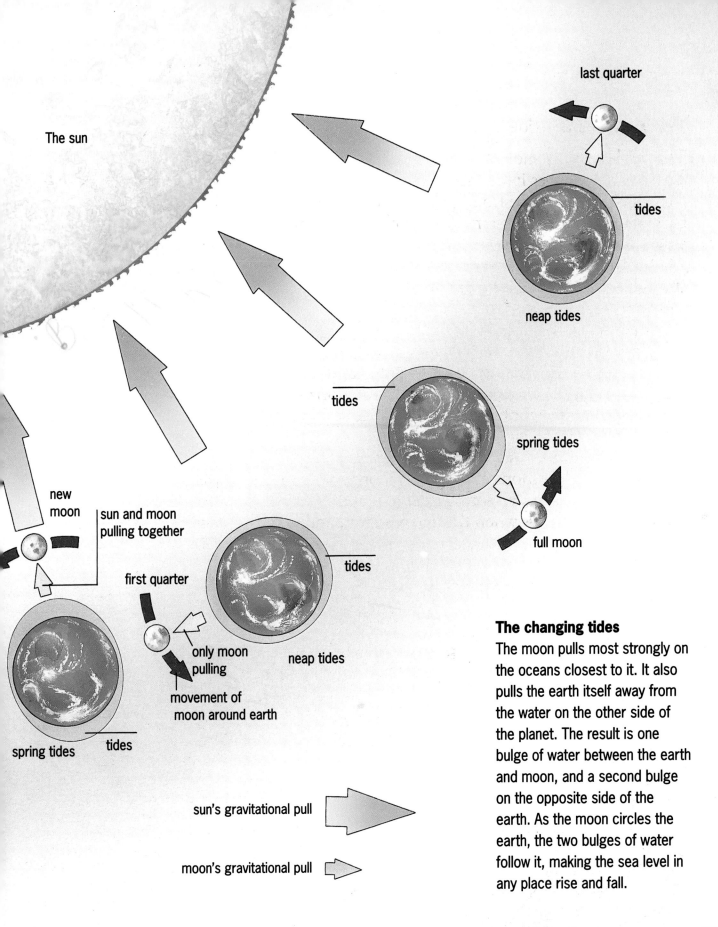

The sun

last quarter

tides

neap tides

tides

spring tides

full moon

new
moon

sun and moon
pulling together

first quarter

tides

only moon
pulling

neap tides

movement of
moon around earth

spring tides   tides

sun's gravitational pull

moon's gravitational pull

The changing tides

The moon pulls most strongly on
the oceans closest to it. It also
pulls the earth itself away from
the water on the other side of
the planet. The result is one
bulge of water between the earth
and moon, and a second bulge
on the opposite side of the
earth. As the moon circles the
earth, the two bulges of water
follow it, making the sea level in
any place rise and fall.

The power of water in nature

The world's coastlines are constantly battered by the sea. Waves churn up the seashore. Depending on the currents, tides, and winds, the waves wash material away from some places and deposit it somewhere else. The constant removal of material from parts of the coast, called coastal erosion, can make cliffs collapse and cause whole villages to fall into the sea.

The highest tides may overwhelm sea defenses and flood vast areas of land, causing great loss of life in some places. The western half of the Netherlands is below sea level. The Dutch people famously protected their country by building land barriers called dikes. In 1953, high tides broke through the dikes and flooded the countryside, killing 1,800 people.

Floods are not always destructive. In ancient Egypt, farmers depended on the flooding of the Nile River to carry rich river mud onto their land and feed their crops. Ice can change the landscape in dramatic ways, too. Glaciers carve out deep U-shaped valleys as they slowly flow down to the sea over many centuries.

FACTFILE

Earthquakes under the sea can produce massive waves called tsunamis. In 1868, an earthquake in the Pacific Ocean produced a tsunami that surged to a height of 46 ft. (14 m) as it hit the coast of Chile. It was so powerful that it carried an American warship 2 mi. (3 km) inland. About 25,000 people died in the resulting flood.

A house collapses into the sea in County Wexford, Ireland, as the constant pounding of waves eat away the cliffs below it.

Inset photo opposite Atlantic waves have carved their way through these shale cliffs on the coast of Cornwall, England, leaving solitary pillars of rock.

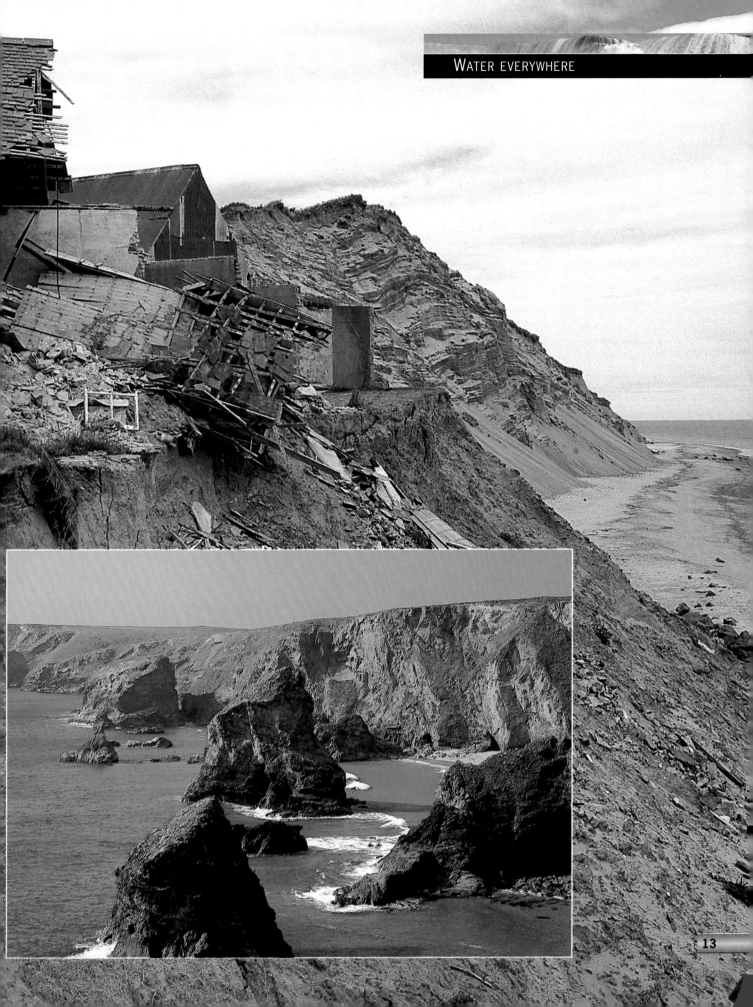

A torrential downpour drenches a tropical beach. Air heavily laden with moisture from the oceans rises over the hot land. As the air rises, its temperature falls. Cool air cannot hold as much moisture as warm air. Eventually, the moisture falls to the land as rain.

FACTFILE

Every year between about April and October, winds blowing across India from the northeast reverse direction. Instead of blowing across the dry Asian landmass, they blow over the Indian Ocean before they reach India. They collect moisture from the ocean and release it as heavy rain on India. Winds that change direction with the seasons like this are called monsoon winds.

How do the oceans affect weather?

The world's oceans have a major effect on our weather and long-term climate. They store some of the sun's heat and spread it around the earth.

Within the oceans there are distinct and generally horizontal flows of seawater in various directions. These ocean currents are caused by a combination of wind currents in the atmosphere, tidal motion, and the emptying of rivers along coasts. There are also vertical flows of seawater caused by warm water rising to the surface, since it is less dense than cold water. There it gives up some of its heat to the air, cools, then sinks back down.

Similarly, as air above the sea warms, it rises. As it does so, it cools, becomes heavier, and sinks back down. Moisture evaporating from the sea is carried upward in the warm air, then condenses to form clouds and eventually falls as rain. This creates the weather cycle.

Ocean Conveyor Belt

The main ocean current, the Great Ocean Conveyor Belt, stretches all around the world and from pole to pole. Deep cold water near the South Pole flows into the warmer Indian and Pacific oceans. As the water warms, it rises and flows west into the Atlantic Ocean. The water then turns north, cools, sinks again, and flows toward the South Pole.

 Warm-water currents

 Cold-water currents

WATER POWER IN HISTORY

Waterwheels

Water was the main source of power for industry for 4,000 years. The first machine built to take advantage of water power was the waterwheel. A waterwheel is a wheel with paddles fixed around its rim. When the wheel is dipped in moving water, the force of water pushing against the paddles turns it. The axle, through the center of the wheel, can be connected to a heavy millstone, to grind grain.

The ancient Egyptians were probably the first to use waterwheels, on the Nile River, as early as 2000 B.C.

A water wheel on the Test River in England. Most water-powered mills and machines disappeared during the nineteenth century as steam engines took over from water power. Most of the waterwheels were dismantled or left to decay, but a few mills with working waterwheels have survived to the present day.

Right: This sixteenth-century French waterwheel operated a series of bellows to force air into furnaces. A complicated series of mechanical links converted the spinning motion of the wheel into a rocking motion that pumped the handles of the bellows up and down.

But the first clear description of a waterwheel was written by the Roman architect Vitruvius in 27 B.C. According to Vitruvius, the waterwheel was in everyday use by then, having been invented by Greek engineers. The Greek geographer Strabo described seeing a water-powered wheel called the hydraletes in 24 B.C. at Cabeira in the Pontus, in present-day Turkey. Most of these early waterwheels drove millstones to make flour, but they were known to have been used for other purposes, too. Some of them operated hammers or bellows in iron forges.

The power of the tides

In places where rivers flowed too slowly to turn a water-wheel, medieval engineers discovered that they could use the rise and fall of the tides as a source of energy. The incoming tide flowed too slowly to be of use, but the water could be stored for use later. The rising waters of the incoming tide were trapped behind wooden gates. As the tide turned, it pushed the gates closed, trapping the water behind them. When the tide had retreated, the water was allowed to flow through the mill wheel.

Tidal mill gates open to let in water.

water trapped behind closed gates

Tidal mill gates open to let trapped water out through mill wheels.

high tide

low tide

The disadvantage of tidal mills

Tidal mills could be used for only a few hours each day at low tide. And because the times of the tides changed each day, the miller's work hours had to change each day, too. In the twelfth century, tidal mills were built on the Adour River near Bayonne, France, and in the estuary of the Deben River in Suffolk, England. They grew in numbers right up to the nineteenth century, when about 100 tidal mills were working in Europe.

Inset opposite An illustration from *Physics in Pictures*, a science book published in 1882. It shows details of the mill wheels and gearing systems in both a windmill and waterwheels.

Above: This tidal power barge anchored in the Thames River in England was used to operate woodworking tools, including a circular saw. A belt carried power from the 6-foot (2-m) diameter wheel underneath the barge to the machinery on the deck.

Steam engines at work

Water power really came into its own with the development of the steam engine in the eighteenth century. When water turns to steam, it expands rapidly and with great force. One quart (1 l) of water produces 343 gal. (1,300 l) of steam. This fact was known in ancient times. Hero of Alexandria made a steam-operated wheel called an aeolipile, but it was never more than an amusing toy. It was never used to do work. The French inventor Denis Papin was the first person to develop machines that used steam to do work. But history remembers Thomas Newcomen as the inventor of the first practical steam engine in 1712.

Left: A nineteenth century diagram of James Watt's steam engine. The new Watt engine was more efficient than Newcomen's and was also very reliable.

Right: Steam from a boiler forced into a piston can be used to turn a wheel, as this diagram shows.

FACTFILE

The first steam locomotive was built by Richard Trevithick in 1804. It pulled a load of ten tons and up to 70 people at a speed of 9 mph (15km/h) along a 9-mi. (15-km) track between an ironworks and a canal in Wales.

A steam locomotive contains a water boiler heated by burning coal. Steam pressure from the boiler turns the wheels.

Step 2   Step 1

steam out

steam in

piston turns machine wheel

steam pushes piston down

piston rod

Steam-powered machines change the world

Newcomen's engine was designed to solve a particular problem. Deep mines often became flooded with water. Newcomen's steam engine was built to pump water out of mines. In 1765, James Watt improved Newcomen's design and used it to drive other types of machinery. By the end of the eighteenth century, hundreds of steam engines had been built. They rapidly transformed Great Britain, and then Europe and America, in a period that became known as the Industrial Revolution.

HARNESSING WATER POWER

An overshot waterwheel like this is three times as efficient as an undershot wheel of the same size because the water's speed and weight both drive the wheel around.

Waterwheel technology

Waterwheels were the first machines that made use of energy from moving water. No one knows exactly where or when the first waterwheels were made, but they were probably invented sometime in the Middle East about 4,000 years ago.

Waterwheels can be vertical or horizontal. Vertical wheels stand upright like a bicycle wheel. When the bottom of a vertical wheel is dipped in water, the force of the water pushing against paddles fixed around the edge pushes it around. This is called an undershot wheel because the water flows underneath it. Its speed depends on the speed of flow of the water.

An overshot vertical wheel turns faster because water runs onto it from above. The water's speed and weight both turn the wheel. The earliest known overshot wheel is shown on a wall painting in the Roman catacombs made in the third century A.D.

A horizontal waterwheel lies flat. It is driven by water falling from above through a pipe or by a jet of water directed at paddles or cups on the wheel rim.

Waterwheels
There are two types of vertical waterwheels—undershot and overshot—and a basic type of horizontal waterwheel.

An overshot vertical water-wheel.

An undershot vertical water-wheel.

A horizontal waterwheel. It lies flat and spins around a vertical axis, or drive rod.

Hydroelectric power

Moving water has energy that can do work. Hydro-electric power stations produce electricity from moving water. The water is guided into a turbine. When it hits the turbine's blades, the force of the water makes the turbine spin. The spinning turbine drives a generator, which converts movement energy into electrical energy.

Generators make more electricity if they spin faster. Turbine speed, and therefore the amount of electricity produced by the generator it drives, depends on water pressure. The greater the water pressure, the faster the turbine spins. Water pressure increases with depth.

At a typical hydroelectric power plant, a deep lake called a reservoir is created by building a dam, or wall, across one end of a valley so that the valley fills up with water. Sluice gates can be opened to allow some of the water to escape so that the dam does not overflow. The water at the bottom of the reservoir is under great pressure because of the weight of water above it.

A hydroelectric installation

dam

valley wall

sluice gate

reservoir

pressure of water pushing down

power plant

generator

Water flows through the channel in the dam.

turbine

Water flows out into the river or canal.

The Glen Canyon Dam across the Colorado River in Arizona is part of a massive hydroelectric installation. It was completed in 1964. The reservoir behind it holds 10.6 billion gal. (40 billion l) of water and stretches across the state line into Utah.

FACTFILE

Hydroelectric power plants provide one fifth of the world's electricity. In developing countries, it provides more—up to 40 percent of the electricity. Almost all the electricity used in Norway is produced by hydroelectric power plants. The world's most powerful power plant is the Itaipu hydroelectric power plant on the Pirana River in South America. It generates 13,320 megawatts—enough electrical power for several cities.

Pumped storage power plants

The demand for electricity constantly changes throughout the day and night. It depends on the time, the day, the weather, and even the times of programs on television! Power plants have to adjust their output to match these changing needs. One type of hydroelectric power plant, called a pumped storage power plant, uses spare electricity from other power plants when demand is low to store water that can be used to produce electricity when demand is high.

At night, when little electricity is needed, a pumped storage power plant pumps water from a reservoir below it to a second reservoir above it. Then during the day, when more electricity is needed, the water is allowed to flow down to the lower reservoir through the power plant's turbines. The turbines drive generators to produce electricity. When the demand for electricity falls again, the generators work in reverse as motors and drive the turbines. The turbines become pumps, which force the water back up to the higher reservoir, ready for the next day.

Opposite: The Ffestiniog complex. Pumped storage power plants need two reservoirs. At Ffestiniog in Wales, they were created by enlarging an existing reservoir and damming a river below the power plant. If there is a sudden surge in demand for electricity, the generators here can produce 360 megawatts within 55 seconds—enough to supply thousands of homes.

The Vigario pumping station in Rio de Janeiro State, Brazil, pumps water uphill through pipes to its upper reservoir. The electricity it generates when it flows back through turbines is carried away by cables held high above the ground by towers called pylons.

When energy is needed, water is allowed to flow down to the turbine room.

The turbines and generators are housed in a vast man-made cave deep in the mountain.

upper reservoir

upper dam

pipes buried in mountainside

water pumped uphill, using spare electricity from other power stations

turbines/pumps

generators/motors

lower reservoir

FACTFILE

There are more than 30 pumped storage power plants in the United States. The world's largest is in Bath County, Virginia. It generates 2,100 megawatts. Together, all U.S. pumped storage power plants produce about 15,000 megawatts.

A dependence on hydroelectricity

Norwegians use more electricity than anyone else in the world. The demand for electricity in Norway has increased by more than half since 1975 and it continues to rise. At the beginning of the twentieth century, most of Norway's energy needs were met by burning wood and coal. Since then, electricity has gradually taken over. Norway could have built any type of power plant, including fossil fuel and nuclear, to satisfy this demand, but the high mountains and heavy rainfall on its western coastline make Norway an ideal place to build hydroelectric power plants. More than 99 percent of electricity in Norway is made from water in this way.

Water gushes from the dam of a hydroelectric power plant at Aursunden in central Norway.

(Figures in TWh [terawatt hours]—trillions of watt hours.)

Norway 119.5

China 151.8

Russia 175.2

Brazil 234.8

United States 276.5

Canada 323.7

Above: A view of the generator room at a hydroelectric power plant in central Norway.

The world's top producers of electricity by water power (based on 1996 figures).

Environmental issues

Some other countries make more electricity from water, but Norway is unique in meeting almost all its electricity needs from hydroelectric power. It costs less than half a Norwegian kroner per kilowatt hour, which is about half the cost of electricity in neighboring Denmark. And hydroelectric power is very kind to the environment. Since no fuel is burned, there are no harmful gases being released into the atmosphere. (Though, of course, fossil fuels were used, and continue to be used, to build the dams and water-power plants.)

Making electricity from waves

Almost any movement of water can be turned into electricity. As the wind blows across the sea, it whips up waves on the surface. The waves roll in toward the land and break on the seashore. Waves travel across the sea's surface, but the water at any particular place is actually bobbing up and down. The energy driving this up and down movement can be converted into electricity. A float sitting on the water's surface bobs up and down with the waves. To generate electricity, this up-down motion has to be converted into a spinning motion that can drive an electricity generator.

Below: A row of Salter's Ducks anchored at sea could generate electricity and send it to the shore by cable. Each "duck" operates a generator as it bobs up and down. Salter's ducks are very efficient. They can change about 90 percent of the wave energy into electricity.

generator rotor turns with up-and-down movement of waves

cutaway view of a Salter's Duck generator unit

This wave generator uses the nodding action of floats to pump air or a fluid such as oil through a turbine. The full-size versions of these generators would be enormous—big enough to land a helicopter on it.

turbine and generator

Fluid reservoir keeps up pressure.

float

water leaves float

water returns to float

moving flap

Bobbing ducks and giant clams

Devices called Salter's Ducks, invented by Dr. Salter of Edinburgh University, Scotland, use the bobbing action of the waves to make electricity in this way. Another device called a clam works in a different way. A series of floating air bags are squeezed as passing waves rise and fall underneath them. Air inside the clam is squeezed from one bag to another. Generators between the bags spin as the air is pushed through. Both these devices are still experimental and small scale, and produce only small quantities of electricity.

Models of wave-energy generators are tested in a water tank before full-size versions are built. All the conditions in the tank are controlled so scientists can measure how good the generators are at using wave energy.

Oscillating water column generators

Waves rolling in toward the land from far out at sea push water against the coast with incredible power. This power can be harnessed in pipes or columns positioned along the coast. When water is pushed in through one end of a pipe, it forces air out the other end. Oscillating water column generators use this effect to make electricity from waves. A chamber with an open top and bottom is set up on a cliff face so that its bottom end is below the water surface.

This blow hole in Australia was formed when water wore a tunnel through the rock. The force of each wave punches water through the funnel-shaped hole and blasts it out of the top. Oscillating water column generators harness the force of the sea in a similar way.

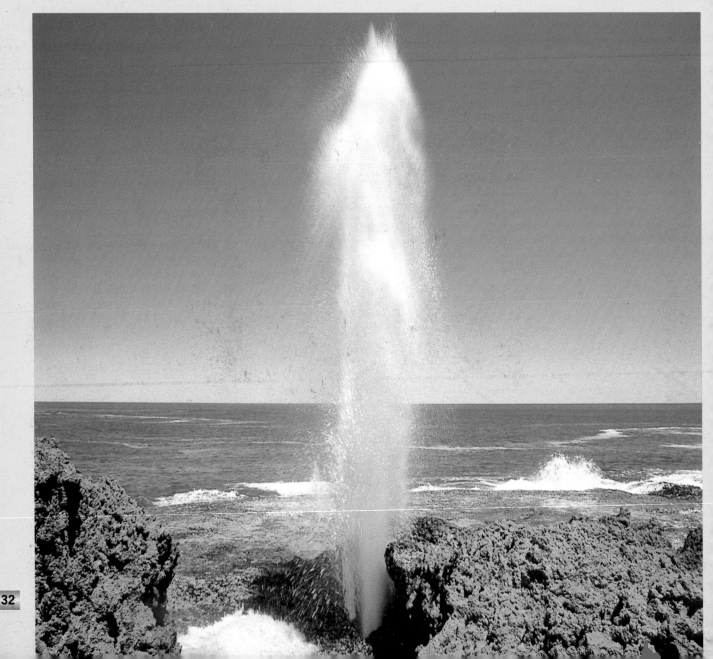

As waves rise and fall, the water level inside the chamber rises and falls too. When the water rises, it pushes air out of the top of the chamber. When the water falls again, it sucks air back in. If a turbine is fitted inside the chamber, the air rushing in and out of the chamber makes it spin. So it is not the waves that generate electricity, it is the air above them.

A few experimental oscillating water column generators have been built. They were so battered by the constant pounding of the waves that most of them were destroyed. But research continues, and some day these power devices may contribute to our supplies of electricity.

An oscillating water column generator on the coast of Norway

A cutaway view inside the Norwegian oscillating water column generator. The turbine (with its blades colored red) is linked to a generator housed within the top of the installation.

Tidal barrages, or barriers

Huge quantities of water move with the tides each day. In some places the tide rushes in and out again fast enough to drive water turbines, but in most places the tides move too slowly. However, they can still be used to generate electricity by using exactly the same method that was used by medieval engineers to build tidal mills 800 years ago. The incoming tide is allowed to flow through sluice gates in a dam or barrage. At high tide, the gates are closed. As the tide ebbs and the water level outside the dam falls, the gates are opened to let the water rush out through turbines.

A threat to wildlife

Tidal power generators work for, at most, only ten hours a day. And the times when they can work keep changing with the tides. Another disadvantage is their effect on the environment. While they are pollution-free, they damage the environment in other ways. The river estuaries where tidal power stations are best built are often important feeding or breeding places for birds. The power plants are likely to drive the birds away.

The East Scheldt sea barrage in the Netherlands.

Birds like this sandpiper
live and breed on open
ground and shorelines in
wet localities such as
estuaries. If power plants
are built in their habitat, it
may drive the birds away.

A wall built across an estuary

The tidal barrage across the mouth of the Rance River at Saint-Malo in France was the first modern tidal power plant of any size to be built. It is still the biggest tidal power plant in the world. Since it was opened in 1966, it has been generating a constant flow of about 240 megawatts of electricity—enough to supply a quarter of a million homes. The river and the open sea are separated by a wall 2,460 ft. (750 m) long. Water can pass through it by means of 24 tunnels. Each tunnel contains a turbine and a generator.

FACTFILE

The Rance River reaches the sea in the bay of Saint-Malo in northwest France where the Channel meets the Atlantic Ocean. Here the difference in height between high and low tide can reach 44 ft. (13.5 m).

The top of the La Rance tidal barrage contains a four-lane highway.

Cutaway view of the tidal barrage on the Rance River

the sea at high tide

roadway

barrage

river basin

the sea at low tide

generators

water flowing out of tunnel in barrage

turbine

sluice gate to control flow

At high tide, water flows from the sea into the river basin.

At low tide, water flows from the river basin to the sea through the barrage tunnels.

The tidal barrage on the Rance River stretches across the river-mouth between Saint-Malo and Dinard. The roadway across the barrage reduces the distance of the trip between the two towns by car by 9 mi. (15 km).

The Gulf of Saint-Malo catches tides flowing in from the Atlantic and funnels them into the mouth of the Rance River, squeezing the water into the narrowing channel and speeding it up. The result is that the tides on the Rance are powerful enough to drive the turbines on both the incoming and outgoing tides.

Most turbines are designed to work with water or steam traveling in one direction only, but the turbines built into the Rance tidal barrage function just as well in whichever direction the water flows. With the tide in full flood, each generator produces up to 10 megawatts of electricity.

Steam turbines

Waterwheels are still in use today, but the real power behind water-driven machinery today is the steam turbine. When water is heated and changed into steam, the steam expands outward at an enormous speed and with great force. This expansion can be put to work.

A steam engine produces an up-down or back-and-forth motion of a piston, which has to be changed into a spinning motion to drive machines. Steam turbines are much simpler. They produce a spinning motion right away, doing away with all the complicated mechanical linkages that go with a steam engine. Unlike waterwheels, which are usually open to the weather, steam turbines must be sealed inside an airtight case so that the high-pressure steam cannot leak out.

Cutaway view of a steam turbine

turbine blades made to spin by steam

turbine shaft rotates about 50 times a second

turbine housing

Steam from the boiler enters the turbine under high pressure.

rotating shaft linked to a generator

Steam is cooled, turns to water and is pumped back to boiler to be turned to steam again.

In the simplest of steam turbines, the speed of steam pushing against the turbine blades makes the drive shaft rotate. In other steam turbines there is an extra set of blades, which are fixed in position. As the steam, still expanding, passes through the fixed blades, it speeds up before hitting the moving blades. This turns the drive shaft harder and faster.

Inside the steam turbine and generator room of a nuclear power plant. Here, the steam pipes are silver colored and the pairs of turbines and generators are red, blue, and yellow.

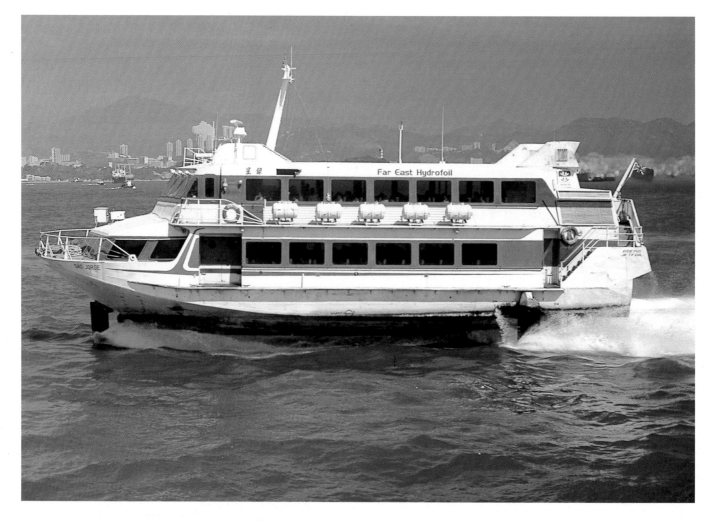

The Boeing Jetfoil is a water-jet-powered hydrofoil. As it speeds up, underwater wings lift its hull out of the water. The engines suck water in through the rear wing and pump it out through the stern.

Water-jet engines

Most ships and boats are powered by engines driving propellers, which are blades fixed to a central rod that is turned at high speed. Propellers can be damaged if they hit the seabed in shallow water. They can also get tangled up in weeds or ropes. Propellers are very dangerous, too, if there are people in the water nearby.

A different type of engine, called a water-jet engine, suffers from none of these disadvantages. Instead of spinning a propeller, the engine pumps out a high-speed jet of water. A large volume of water is sucked in through the bottom of the craft, speeded up by pumps, and concentrated into a much narrower and faster jet.

High-speed sea craft

The same water jet can also be used to steer the craft, by swiveling the jet to one side or the other. The world's fastest and largest car ferries are powered by water-jet engines. They use the same jet engines as fighter planes and airliners. Instead of producing a jet of air, they drive pumps that move amazing amounts of water. When the HSS 1500 car ferry's engines are running at full power, they pump out 22,450 gal. (85,000 l) of water (enough to fill 250 bathtubs) every second!

A jet ski skims across shallow water, using its water-jet engines.

An oceangoing ferry such as a SeaCat sucks in water through the bottom of the craft and pumps water out through steering water jets at the back. The craft can reach speeds of 42 knots, about 47 mph (76km/h).

pump units

water jet outlet

water intake

F A C T F I L E

The natural world discovered water-jet propulsion millions of years before people built water-jet engines. Flattened shellfish called scallops swim by repeatedly snapping their shells closed to squirt out jets of water. Many jellyfish move around by gently pulsing their bodies to push against water.

Kawasaki

Water jets are used in gold prospecting. In Alaska, water jets cut through the frost-hard ground and wash out gravels that may contain gold.

F ACTFILE

Jets of water from hoses have been used to wash out ore-bearing gravels and sands for decades. However, using a water jet to cut materials like metal and wood is a much more recent development. This type of water-jet cutting was invented in 1968 by Norman Franz in the United States.

Water-jet tools

Water in nature can carve caves out of rock, bring down cliffs, and wash away roads and bridges. Water jets are sometimes used in a similar way in mining, to cut through earth containing valuable minerals and wash it down into a collection area. China clay is extracted in this way. More powerful water jets cut through coal.

When water is concentrated into a thin jet, it can cut through tough materials in a highly controlled way. A high-pressure jet of water can clean something by blasting off the dirt. The black crust of grime caused by years of air pollution is stripped off stone buildings in this way. If the pressure is boosted still further, it can cut through the material itself, not just dirt on its surface. The most advanced water-cutting tools work at water pressures of sufficient force to break reinforced concrete. Harsh rocky particles are added to the water to improve its cutting power. Water-jet tools can now drill or cut through such materials as steel and titanium.

A compressor is used to pump water to a nozzle, which sprays it out as a jet of dirt-removing droplets.

THE FUTURE OF WATER POWER

Harnessing the heat of oceans

Tidal power and wave power are at an early stage in their development. But as fossil fuels begin to run out, we are likely to build more tidal barrages across river estuaries and more wave-power generators along coasts. There may also be machines called OTECs (Ocean Thermal Energy Converters) making electricity in warm tropical seas. Ocean temperature falls with depth. The surface may be as warm as 77° F (25° C), while deeper water is nearly freezing. This difference in temperature is used to evaporate a liquid and so drive a turbine.

In an OTEC machine, warm surface water evaporates a liquid such as ammonia. The vapor drives a turbine and is then changed back to a liquid by cold water pumped up from the depths.

crew quarters with helipad on the roof

warm-water intake

warm surface water

warm-water outlet

condenser

cold-water outlet

turbine

intake pipe: 100 ft. (30 m) in diameter and up to 3,300 ft. (1,000 m) long

cold deep water

cold-water riser pipe

anchorage cable

A handful of small experimental OTECs have been built, but so far no large commercial OTEC machines have been constructed.

Power generators in the sea have to withstand constant pounding from waves and tides. Plants and animals can make their homes on and inside any machine, and seawater could damage it or make it less effective. But as all renewable energy sources are investigated more in the future, these problems will eventually be overcome. In the meantime, conventional hydroelectric projects and low-technology, inexpensive water mills will continue to be built.

Controllers in a future power station look out over rows of wave power generators. Their computers monitor the sea conditions and the power output of the generators.

A chain of bobbing ducks spans part of the estuary mouth, converting wave energy into electricity. Behind the ducks are oscillating water column generators.

A wind-assisted cargo ship heads for the open sea.

GLOSSARY

Atmosphere The gases that surround the earth, containing mostly nitrogen (78 percent) and oxygen (21 percent).

Atom The smallest particle of matter that can take part in chemical reactions.

Billion One thousand million.

Boiler A water tank designed for heating water and turning it into steam.

Carbon dioxide A gas containing carbon and oxygen that forms 0.03 percent of the earth's atmosphere.

Clam A shellfish; also the name of a type of wave power generator.

Dam A barrier built to hold back water.

Dike A land barrier built to keep the sea from flooding low-lying land, especially in the Netherlands.

Estuary The tidal mouth of a river where it meets the sea.

Evaporate Change from a liquid into a gas.

Fossil fuel Coal, oil, and natural gas—fuels formed in prehistoric times from the decay of plants and microscopic animals.

Generator A machine designed to change movement energy into electrical energy.

Glacier A large mass of ice formed from snow on land. The deepest layers of snow are compressed (squeezed) by the weight of snow above them and change into hard glacier ice.

Global warming An increase in the earth's temperature that may be happening because of human activities.

Great Ocean Conveyor Belt The main ocean current that drives seawater around the world.

Horizon The line where the earth and the sky seem to meet.

Hurricane A violent circular storm that forms over water in the Atlantic Ocean, especially in the Caribbean Sea.

Hydroelectric power Electricity generated by the energy of falling water.

Hydrofoil A type of boat with underwater wings that lift its hull out of the water when it accelerates.

Hydrogen The lightest and most common of all gases in the universe.

Kilo- A prefix meaning 1,000 as in kilowatt, kilometer.

Kilowatt A unit of electrical power meaning 1,000 watts.

Kilowatt-hour A unit of electrical energy equivalent to 1,000 watts used for one hour.

Mega- A prefix meaning one million.

Megawatt A unit of electrical power meaning one million watts—enough to supply the total needs of a family house.

Monsoon A seasonal wind over India and south Asia blowing from the southwest in the summer and from the northeast in the winter.

Neap tide A small tide that occurs at the moon's first and third quarters.

Oscillating wave column generator A type of electricity generator that changes the up-down motion of sea waves into electricity.

OTEC Ocean Thermal Energy Converter. A machine for making electricity by using the difference in temperature in water at different depths.

Overshot Waterwheel One powered by water falling on it from above.

Piston The part of an engine that slides up and down inside a close-fitting cylinder.

Reservoir A large natural or artificial lake used as a supply of water.

Salter's Duck A wave power generator that produces electricity from the bobbing action of waves.

Sluice gate A gate fitted to a water channel to control the amount of water passing through it.

Spring tide A high tide that occurs at the new moon or full moon when the sun, moon, and earth are in line.

Steam engine An engine powered by steam pressure.

Tidal power plant A power plant that generates electricity by using the tides.

Tidal range The difference in sea level between high and low tides.

Tide The daily rise and fall in sea level caused by the gravitational pull of the moon and sun.

Tsunami A large, powerful, and destructive wave caused by an underwater earthquake.

Turbine A machine that uses a moving fluid such as water or oil, or a vapor like steam, to spin a wheel or drum with blades set around its edge.

Typhoon A violent storm in the Pacific Ocean.

Undershot Waterwheel One driven by water flowing underneath it.

Water cycle The circulation of water from land and sea to the atmosphere and back to the land and sea again.

Water jet engine A type of engine that propels a ship or water bike by means of a high-pressure jet of water.

Water mill A grain mill in which the mill stone is driven by a water wheel.

Waterwheel A wheel driven by running water.

FURTHER INFORMATION

Books to read

Chandler, Gary & Kevin, Graham. *Protecting Our Air, Land, & Water* (Making a Better World). New York: 21st Century Books, 1996.

Cossi, Olga. *Water Wars: The Fight to Control and Conserve Nature's Most Precious Resource.* Parsippany, NJ: Silver Burdett Press, 1993.

Dolan, Edward F. *Our Poisoned Waters*. New York: Cobblehill Books, 1997.

Edmonds, Alex. *Acid Rain* (Closer Look At). Brookfield, CT: Copper Beech, 1997.

Gardner, Robert. *Experimenting with Water* (Venture Science Experiments and Projects). Danbury, CT: Franklin Watts, 1993.

Morgan, Adrian and Morgan, Sally. *Water* (Designs in Science). New York: Facts on File, 1994.

Ocko, Stephanie. *Water: Almost Enough for Everyone.* New York: Atheneum Books, 1995.

Power and energy consumption

Power is the measurement of how quickly energy is used. It is measured in joules per second, or watts. An electric iron might need 1,000 watts to work, but a portable radio might need only 10 watts. The energy needed to keep the radio going for one hour would run the iron for only six minutes, because the iron uses up energy ten times faster than the radio. The diagram to the right compares the power ratings of household electrical goods and of homes and power stations.

A power plant produces several millions of watts.

Electricity needs of a family house total a few thousand watts.

Washing machine
2,500 watts
Electric iron
1,000 watts
Microwave oven
850 watts
Lightbulb
100 watts
Portable radio
10 watts

INDEX